# Kia ora Postie

This book is dedicated to
the posties of New Zealand

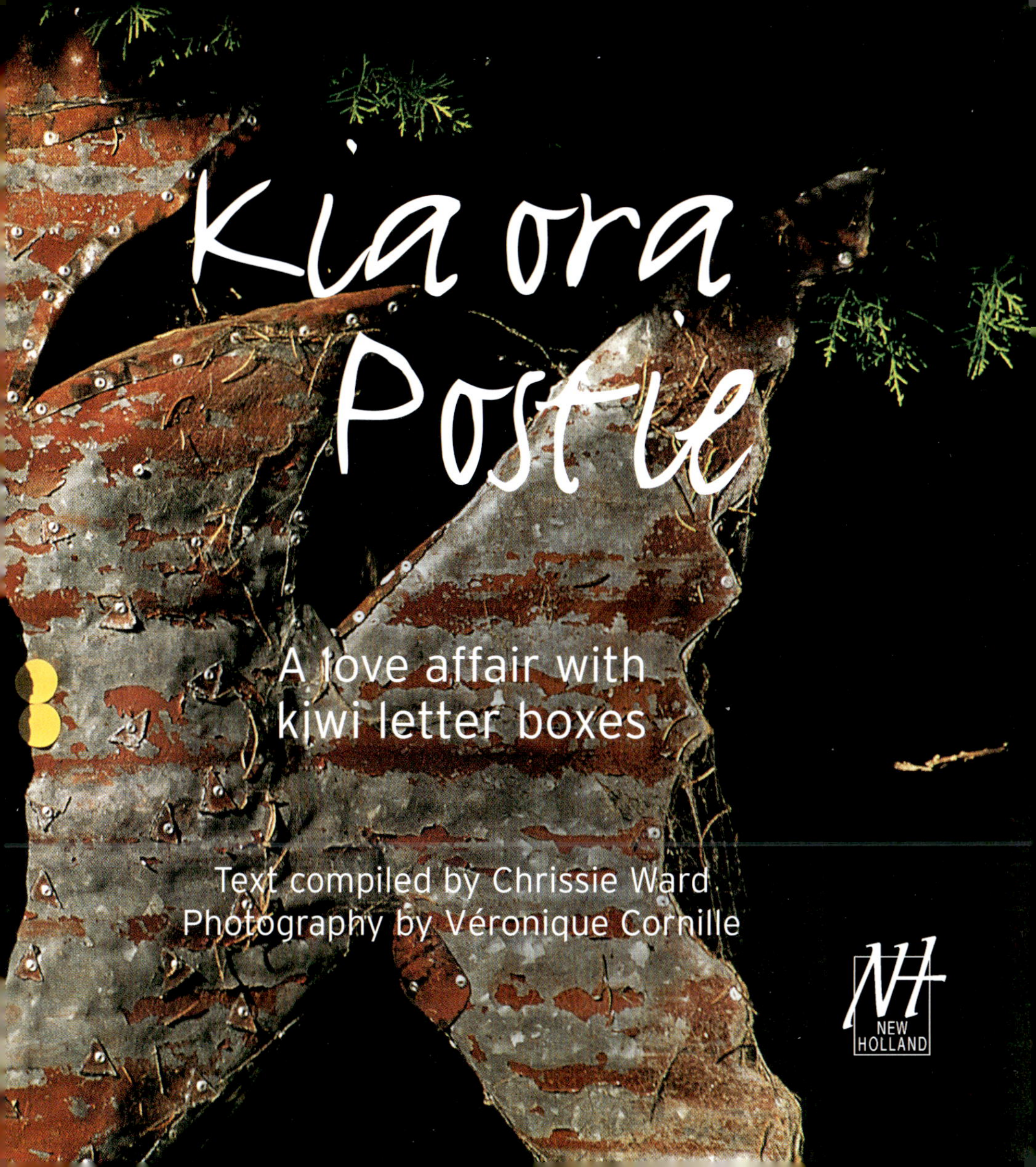

# Kia ora Postie

## A love affair with kiwi letter boxes

Text compiled by Chrissie Ward
Photography by Véronique Cornille

NH
NEW HOLLAND

# Introduction

## Kia ora – greetings – postie!

New Zealand is among the few countries (the USA, Australia and Norway are others) where mail is delivered to a letter box at the gate, rather than to the door. Many overseas visitors will be impressed by the trust that is implied in having mail left in boxes on the street.

Organised post started here in 1840. By coincidence, that was the year that penny postage became established in Britain, but it would be another fifteen years before New Zealand had its own postage stamps. Our system of mail delivery developed in a pragmatic fashion. Early European settlers in towns had to call at the local post office to collect mail over the counter. There would have been a great crush when the monthly ships from Britain arrived, but at least mail was received fairly regularly. It was a different matter in rural districts, as some of the stories in this book illustrate.

Coastal settlements could receive mail by ship. When settlers set up sheep stations or runs inland they would group together to share the cost of a regular letter delivery from a post office, often quite distant, into their area. The mailman carried an 'open' (unsealed) bag with letters to all stations, and settlers would take out their own mail and put outward letters into it. This service was subsidised by the Post Office. At first, mail was delivered by horse and rider, but with improving roads the use of vehicles speeded up delivery.

The postmaster and his faithful spaniel wait for the next train outside their small Post & Telegraph Office at Wakefield, Nelson Province, circa 1900. Picture courtesy Tasman Bays Heritage Trust/Nelson Provincial Museum, Tyree Studio Collection 114892/5

In the towns, meanwhile, post office messengers would deliver letters by hand around the central business districts if they had any spare time. In July 1878 the messengers' role as 'letter carriers' was formalised when the first official branch delivery system was set up at Sydenham in Christchurch. Similar systems were gradually introduced in more places, and over-the-counter collection of mail eventually came to an end.

The letter carriers delivered newspapers and parcels as well as letters, and in April 1919 they were renamed postmen. They delivered to the front door, notifying the householder at first by a double knock and later by blowing a whistle. Some older buildings still have brass or cast-iron slots in their doors for receiving mail, as remains standard in Britain and other European countries.

Calling at the door took up a great deal of time, as well as being hard on the posties' feet. From August 1907, householders were required to place a letter box at their gate if the front door was more than 50 yards from the road. This regulation was taken a step further in January 1913, when all new houses had to have a letter box at the gate. With the shortage of manpower during the First World War, delivery to the gate became compulsory for everyone.

It took longer to get letter boxes established in country areas. The Rural Delivery system operating today was modelled on the American system, which began in 1896. Little progress was made in New Zealand until 1912, when Canadian-made letter boxes were imported and sold to anyone living on a rural mail route. This allowed the Post Office to start insisting that boxes be properly located at the roadside. From 1914 locally made boxes were provided.

The only letter box on Takapourewa/Stephen's Island, a remote wildlife sanctuary in Cook Strait. Every month the Department of Conservation delivers supplies and mail to the ranger and his wife – but never to the box high up on the hill! One of the former rangers who obviously had a sense of humour placed it there.

Special attachments known as 'flags' – levers with a rectangle at the end – were introduced in December 1915. When raised, they indicate to the mail carrier that there is mail to collect. The use of flags was made mandatory in 1916. It is not known what the first flags were made of, but modern ones are metal. They should be (but often aren't) painted red.

During the 1930s and '40s, postmen wore the same uniform of dark blue serge during summer and winter. All posties were male until World War Two. Then women had to take over the roles previously held by men, and blue serge skirts became acceptable. Today's posties, whether male or female, dress for comfort and safety.

Letter boxes may now be compulsory, but there is no rule to say what they should look like. Many people take the opportunity to use their imagination and artistic talent, and turn a mundane article into an individual statement.

On the simplest level, store-bought boxes can be decorated with paint or accessories, or have succulent gardens planted on top. More ambitious householders create sculptures of animals, elegant forms or fantastical shapes. Recycling is popular. With a bit of ingenuity, anything – gas cylinders, obsolete machinery, drums, old ticket machines, driftwood or logs, even microwave ovens – can be turned into a letter box.

In country districts, or in towns where there are steep and narrow streets, letter boxes are placed together so as to be convenient for the postie, making interesting groups. In some communities, a friendly competition seems to develop between householders as to who can have the most unusual letter box. Naturally, they are all very proud of their creations. The photographs in this book illustrate the wealth of inventiveness that can be seen on any street or country road anywhere in Aotearoa New Zealand.

Chrissie Ward
Nelson

NO CIRCULA

# slot shot

'After the first few exasperating days on the road, I began to enjoy the intriguing game of learning to pop letters through the slots of the boxes without stopping my bicycle to do it. … The first time you can put a letter into a box without having to stop is a major victory, a milestone in your postal career. Mine was a small letter, and the opening of the letter-box – the very last on my round – was large enough to take a good-sized leg of mutton. Nevertheless, the feat was a triumph which gave me a warm pleasant feeling of achievement. What a pity it was the last box! I was quite sorry I had no more letters to practise on. I looked up and down the street. No one was near. So I gently retrieved the letter, rode back a few yards, turned round and did it again.'

From *Whistles for the Postie* by Freda Bream (Collins, 1972)

19
BURROWS

17-697
17-707
17-717
17-727
17-698
17-708
17-718
17-728
17-699
17-709
17-719
17-729

117

# Bush Telegraph

On 18 June 1862 the *Lyttelton Times* announced proudly: 'The whole of the telegraph wire has been stretched and fixed between Christchurch and Lyttelton. It is probable that the first telegrams will be sent to-day. The opening of the first telegraph line in New Zealand must be considered as an epoch in the history of the Colony. It is no small gratification that Canterbury can claim the credit of being the first Province to introduce this last great wonder of civilization in New Zealand.'

Before most people had telephones, the fastest means of communicating was the telegraph, by which coded electrical signals were sent along transmission lines. The spread of telegraphy happened rapidly in the South Island. Progress in the North Island was slower, as many Māori objected to the poles and lines passing over their land. The stretch between Opunake and New Plymouth was particularly difficult, and for some years there was the absurd situation of telegrams to and from New Plymouth being carried on horseback.

STRONG

72A

MAIL

RODGER & ALI
BRODIE

# Don't Forget the Fish

Noel's first job, at age fifteen, was in Woodville in 1956 as a telegram delivery boy. He also acted as a relieving postman. Sometimes he had to clear the collection boxes, which at the time were fixed to telegraph poles. One day, when he came to empty a box he was surprised to find a 'slat' – a piece of plywood the same size as an envelope. That's not a letter, he thought, and replaced it in the box. Another few boxes on, there was another of the wooden things. 'What the heck?' he thought, and chucked it back.

Later that day he was approached by his supervisor and asked, 'Did you clear all the boxes?'

'Yes, sir,' Noel replied.

'Did you clear them completely?'

'Yes, sir.'

'Where are the fish?'

'Fish? What fish?' Noel was bewildered.

'The fish – the wooden fish!'

'Oh, those! They weren't letters, so I just left them.'

'You are supposed to bring them back!'

'Well, nobody told me,' said Noel.

It was then that Noel realised his supervisor's cunning way of checking whether the posties were doing their jobs properly. And on every subsequent Thursday afternoon, when the supervisor put bicycle clips on his trousers, Noel would smile to himself. The supervisor was going for a long ride around town, planting 'fish' to catch lazy posties.

www.laughingfishstudio.co.nz

EMERGENCY
SERVICES No
458
457
453

454
451
JENKINS

DON &
CAROL
DUFFY

Anchor
Fresh Milk
Anchor
Milkman
only
THE MAIL

# Special Delivery

'In the early days (1890s) the so-called road was little better than a clay track through the bush. Honest Tom drove his own coach. Often he would have to cut a track through fallen timber, or make one round slips and washouts, or find a way along the side to avoid getting stuck in the deep mud in the middle of the road. … However, although it would sometimes be 10 or later at night when he reached his destination, Tom would always manage somehow or other to get through. In fact, it became almost a legend in the district, that no matter what conditions were like, as long as Tom was on the coach, settlers could be sure of getting their mails and supplies.'

From *Tales of the Mails* by Lester Masters (Hart Print, 1959)

343

Junk Mail
SUNDAY
187

26

ONEILL
LEESTON
73

THANK YOU
CASSETTA
PER
LE LETTERE
REGIE POSTE

# Lackadaisically Yours

Gisborne's first letter carrier, Albert Fyson, was appointed in 1879. His initial contract didn't specify that he should go out on a delivery round, so he didn't bother. Instead, he would put a bundle of letters in his coat pocket and stroll up and down the main street, hoping to come across the addressees. Any letters for Maori were piled up on the counter, and the recipients were told to sort through the heap.

Sourced from *Historic Poverty Bay and the East Coast, N.I., N.Z.* by J. A. Mackay (1949, 3rd impression 1973)

SNOOK

MATARAE
MERCER
EMERGENCY
SERVICES No
2108

PRINGLE
EMERGENCY SERVICES No
412
The Nelson Mail

30

14

Jim & Gabrielle Ponsford

# A Postie's Best Friend

An unusual way of delivering the mail is described in the 1863 diary of E. R. Chudleigh while staying at Castle Hill Station, Canterbury:

'I must mention a wonderful dog here. When the river is high, this dog has the letters strapped to his back in an oilskin. He goes over the river and then on a mile and a half, gives up his letters, and returns with the answers. He is a large, rough collie, hailed as "Postman".'

From *The Road to the West Coast: A history of the road over Arthur's Pass* by Ivan D. Taylor (Heritage Press, 2005)

102

# On Boxes and Birds

Odd letter boxes don't always find favour with posties: '... to put a letter through the slot, one has first to locate the letter-box. This was not always as simple as it sounds. There were boxes of all varieties: boxes in the shape of little houses, round boxes, square boxes, empty biscuit tins, old oil drums, kerosene tins, apple cases, cardboard cartons, backless boxes with a tilt, so that letters placed in them would immediately slide out the other side ... boxes delicately balanced, so that when touched they would collapse to the ground ... boxes so well hidden that no new postman could find them unaided, boxes labelled "Don't use", and boxes too full of gardening tools, empty jam jars, or (in one instance) shoes, to hold all the mail as well.

'I wondered why one household had bought a wooden starlings' nest as a letter-box. But it seemed adequate enough. I simply rolled up the letters one by one and pushed them through the little round hole, until I found out one day that the box was exactly what it claimed to be – a starlings' nest. The letter-box was two yards away, in heavy disguise behind a privet hedge. The starlings had apparently made the same mistake as I, for there were no feathered occupants as long as I was on that round.'

From *Whistles for the Postie* by Freda Bream (Collins, 1972)

494

MURROW
211
209

199
NO CIRCULARS
RIDGEN
213
NO CIRCULARS
SPRING
NO CIRCULARS

# Stretching a Point

'Letter-boxes were required by the Post Office to be situated within three feet of the front gate. But a lot can happen in three feet. As long as the back of the box is accessible to the owner to collect his mail, he is apt to forget about its front, or else he neglects it deliberately, as being entirely the postman's side of the problem. You may have to hurdle a tricycle, a couple of packing cases and a watering can, before you can even extend your arm far enough to reach the slot.'

From *Whistles for the Postie* by Freda Bream (Collins, 1972)

240

KEYS
KEYS
8

3
NO ADVERTISING
MATERIAL
THANK YOU

MORANTE.MANSSON.MACLEOD.

EMERGENCY
SERVICES No
2110

NO JUNK
MAIL
26

# Foxed by the Box

'When I got mail delivery at home in early 2005 and I gave up my post office box, it was the first time in my life I'd had a real letter box. And I discovered the joys of the red flag, and having my mail picked up. When I explained how it worked to my daughter she told me about her flatmate – home schooled and brought up on a remote farm – who, when he moved into their flat in Auckland, complained one day that his mail hadn't been picked up. She discovered he'd presumed town boxes worked the same way. Despite being puzzled by the lack of a flag, he'd just put his outward mail in the box and assumed it would be collected. And was then baffled and slightly hurt when four days later it was still there!'

Lesley
Maungatapere

30c

POST OFFICE
LETTER BOX
154
CLEARED AT
MONDAY TO SATURDAY
10AM

57
FLAT i
NO CIRCULARS
PLEASE

NO CIRCULARS

21

# Sarah Ann's Woes

Together with her husband and three young sons, Sarah Ann Walker emigrated from England in 1859, settling on a farm near Temuka. The marriage was very unhappy, Sarah Ann was homesick, and corresponding with her family in England seems to have been all that kept her going. Making great efforts to catch the mail herself, she was irritated by the attitude of some postmen, as she records in several letters:

**July 1861**

'… the fresh (postman) is very careless about giving people their letters. We have just got 4 papers from you and 2 of them have been there 2 months.'

**Sept 1873**

'… There are so many of the same name here that it is not safe to send any (letters) unregistered for we are further away than the others and the postman gives the first that comes. He does not care about it at all …'

**Sept 1882**

'I am writing this in great haste. I did not know the mail went out today so I can only say a few words … I could not take the trap, so I am to walk to post this, 12 miles. I don't know if I shall be on time, for the roads are ankle deep in mud, but I shall try …'

Letter extracts courtesy South Canterbury Museum, Timaru

FIVE IS ALIVE

5
MAIL
ASE

PIPPA BOWKER-NAPP
ANTHEA BOWKER
JOANNA BOWKER
GREG NAPP
SAMUEL BOWKER-NAPP

12

# Helen's journey

During the late 1990s, Maggie worked as a postie in Nelson while also running a motel. A guest called Helen had just arrived from Christchurch one evening when she received an urgent telephone call. Her mother was seriously ill in hospital. She had to get back – but how? The last flight to Christchurch had gone.

Maggie thought fast. Perhaps the mail centre could help? She telephoned the shift manager and explained the problem.

'The mail truck's leaving in five minutes,' he said. 'Bring her down now!'

Helen travelled in the truck to the airport at Blenheim, where she and the mail transferred to a van and set off for Christchurch. She asked the driver how often he had a passenger.

'Occasionally,' he replied, 'but we usually run out of things to talk about before we've left Blenheim.'

'We're doing pretty well, then, aren't we? Here we are at Kaikoura, and we're still talking!'

They arrived at Christchurch fifteen minutes after midnight. The Nelson Mail Centre had arranged for a taxi to be waiting at the depot, and Helen was rushed straight to the hospital. She was grateful to be able to spend precious time with her mother before her death a week later.

# The Authors

Nelson-born **Chrissie Ward** studied haphazardly at three New Zealand universities, and in 1975 left on an 'overseas experience' that lasted for 23 years. She began writing fiction while running a market garden in the Shetland Islands, off the north coast of Scotland. When she returned to New Zealand in 1998 she edited *Dear Lizzie: A Kiwi Soldier Writes From The Battlefields Of World War One* (a collection of her grandfather's letters, published by HarperCollins). Chrissie has had many short stories and articles published online and in print in New Zealand and overseas. On returning to live in Nelson, she fell in love with customised letter boxes and was inspired to create this book.

**Véronique Cornille**'s images draw their influence from three cultures and *Flandria*, the family farm at Port Waikato/Te Puaha o Waikato, her turangawaewae. Her Flemish family were, and still are, part of the Ngāti Tipa people there. Swimming and whitebaiting in the Waikato River, surfing in the Tasman Sea and being part of a strong local culture that embraced tikanga Māori were the foundation for her works in natural and cultural heritage. She is the author of *Nelson Alive*, a photographic tribute to the region in which she lives, and is the photographer for *The Outside Table* (published by the Suter Art Gallery), a book celebrating food, recipes and the outdoor lifestyle.

**Acknowledgements**
The authors would like to thank the creators of the wonderful letter boxes featured in this book. Special thanks go to Robin Startup for providing information about New Zealand postal history.

First published in 2006 by New Holland Publishers (NZ) Ltd
Auckland • Sydney • London • Cape Town

www.newhollandpublishers.co.nz

218 Lake Road, Northcote, Auckland, New Zealand
14 Aquatic Drive, Frenchs Forest, NSW 2086, Australia
86–88 Edgware Road, London W2 2EA, United Kingdom
80 McKenzie Street, Cape Town 8001, South Africa



ISBN-13: 978 1 86966 140 3
ISBN-10: 1 86966 140 0

Managing editor: Matt Turner
Design: Gina Hochstein

A catalogue record for this book is available from the National Library of New Zealand

1 3 5 7 9 10 8 6 4 2

Colour reproduction by Pica Digital Pte Ltd, Singapore
Printed in China at Everbest Printing Co